MARIA NEPHELE

A POEM IN TWO VOICES

ODYSSEUS ELYTIS

Translated from the Greek by
Athan Anagnostopoulos

Houghton Mifflin Company Boston
1981

Library of Congress Cataloging in Publication Data

Elytēs, Odysseas, date
Maria Nephele : a poem in two voices.

I. Anagnostopoulos, Athan. II. Title.
PA5610.E43M313 889′.132 81-2691
ISBN 0-395-29465-7 AACR

Printed in the United States of America

V 10 9 8 7 6 5 4 3 2 1

Portions of this book have appeared in *The Paris Review* and *WorldPaper*.

CONTENTS

III

TRANSLATOR'S INTRODUCTION

PUBLISHED IN Athens in December 1978, *Maria Nephele* enjoyed an unprecedented success, particularly with young readers. Eighteen years before its publication, Elytis had begun to compose the forty-five poems that make up the book, at the time he was finishing his celebrated *Axion Esti* (1959). The poet prefixed two epigraphs to his new book. The first is taken from the New Testament and warns that the reader is not resisting evil; the second, from Elytis's first book of poems, *Orientations* (1939), informs us that there are two aspects of his self. Nearly forty years later, in *Maria Nephele*, Elytis shapes these two aspects of himself into the personae of his poem: Maria Nephele and the Antiphonist—the respondent, who is the poet himself. This inherent duality emanates both from the essential unity of the poet—a unity that, although irrevocable, is never static—and his constant capacity for renewal and expansion.

The name *Maria Nephele* is laden with mythological significance. Maria is the name of Christ's Holy Mother, man's mediator with God, and it is also a common name for girls. The literal meaning of the word *nephele* is cloud; its metaphorical meaning is grief, death. In Greek mythology, Nephele was the name given Hera when she assumed the form of a cloud. In Aristophanes' play *The Clouds*, the Nephelae represent the new, natural deities, the new trends in educational, cultural, and philosophical thought. Socrates describes them as able to assume any form they wish, reflect the things they see on earth, and smoothly fuse into new forms.

Elytis has characterized *Maria Nephele* as a strange kind of poem that belongs to his third creative period and that is more complex in structure than *Axion Esti*: "In it a girl speaks. Her words are on the left side of the page and the poet's reactions on the right. Yet it is not a dialogue but two monologues side by side." Maria Nephele, the girl who speaks in the poem, is both a mythical woman and a real person known to the poet: "I met this young woman in real life, and I suddenly wanted to write something very different from the *Axion Esti*. Therefore, I made this young woman speak in my poem and express her world view, which is that of the young generation of today."

Maria Nephele is a revolutionary, "the puma of the public streets," the "cultural revolution." She listens to records lying on the floor, chain smokes, wears multicolored skirts and bell-bottom pants; her soul is a "mongolfier of regrets." Maria Nephele is nervous, frustrated, and perplexed in a world devastated by war, torn by political and social strife, manipulated by bourgeois ideology, and stifled by technology and consumerism. She is sad and pale, "beautiful like a natural phenomenon." "I try to understand her," Elytis says, "by having us speak in parallel monologues. My conclusion in this poem is that we search basically for the same things, but along different routes."

Maria Nephele believes in the sanctity of life and the beauty of the body. Like the mythical Nephele, she undergoes many metamorphoses, changing shape according to the times and circumstances. Endowed with divine powers, she can turn into rain, lightning, and thunder, or become Iris, the messenger of the gods, the goddess of the rainbow: "green in the big novelty stores / violet in the underworld cafés / red in the funerals of the poor / and blue in the sleep of infants." Her prophetic powers enable her, like Aeschylus' Cassandra, to see the death before the murder, the spilled blood before the cries of agony and the deathly blows. Drunk in an underground bar, she seeks to avenge herself like the outcast Electra, a deprived and humiliated princess "shorn and ugly," who has "graze[d] the swine / for centuries now, outside the walls." She calls on "the Queen with the cobwebs" for help, or awaits "an unknown brother," an Orestes who will save her. Maria Nephele draws her power from the harmony, purity, and justice that imbues the natural world. She identifies with natural phenomena and the forces of nature: the distant influence of the stars, the flowing currents of the sea, the moon's gravitation, and her elements, rain and lightning.

There is an indomitable spirit in Maria Nephele's search for self-knowledge and her pursuit of justice. She is ready to exorcise "the evil spirits of this world" and restore the dignity of life to its original, unadulterated state: "Let's give the earth back to our feet . . . / there's need for a tigress' leap into ideas," she cries out in despair, loveless and joyless as she wanders "like an angel . . . over the abyss." Maria Nephele is endowed with a keen mind and is a threat to established values: "she gleams like a knife." This real or fabulous Maria Nephele — Iris, Cassandra, Helen, Electra, Diotima, Djenda — strives to liberate herself from the shackles of prejudice and conventionality: "Maria Nephele lives at the antipodes of Ethics / she is full of ethos." Her dreams and fantasies express her true essence and allow her to address herself to lofty emotions and the freedom of the individual: "We are the negative of dream / that's why we appear black and white / and live decay / in a minute reality." Her mysterious and divine origin allows her to "sing and chant Man's Unwritten Words," as she proceeds "dodecaphonic / nerve-racking / lightninglike / beautiful." She reaches beyond the rational: The invisible becomes visible through the senses, not through cerebral notions; the visible world offers an imperfect degree of consciousness. We, with our limited perceptions, tend to forget that "the house is not always smaller than the mountain / man is not always bigger than the flower."

As her names indicate, Maria Nephele represents both divine grace and change: she is at once formed and unformed, like water, her element, which is also the poet's element. Water is life-giving; the essence; that which actually germinates life: "All things a waterdrop / of beauty trembling on the lashes." She has the power to unify ideas, images, and themes of all times and places, ancient or modern. She is the midwife who will help the poet look at the miracle of life with fresh eyes, "for the benefit of the authenticity of human vision." Maria Nephele is the mediator between the poet and the world. The poet needs her intuitive wisdom in order to move outside his own boundaries. He must reach into the heartbeat of life and refresh his vision, so that he may perceive truth: "my fingernails will tear into your flesh / truth — don't they say so? — is painful / and needs you to know your blood / needs your wounds."

With Maria Nephele as guide, the poet abandons his seclusion. Unlike the poet of *Sun the First* (1943), *Axion Esti* (1959), *Six and One Remorses for the Sky* (1960), *The Sovereign Sun* (1971), and *The Light Tree* (1971), who delved into the mysteries of nature, the metaphysics of light and love, the marvels of the Aegean Sea, and the struggles of his homeland for survival and freedom, the Antiphonist sets out deliberately to explore new frontiers of human experience and existence by venturing into the "Forest of Men," by joining his fellow man in the jungle of the modern megalopolis: "Poetry O my saint — forgive me / but I need to stay alive / to cross over to the other side; / anything would be preferable / to my slow assassination by the past." The city is the natural setting for new ideas, trouble, protest, and social, political, and cultural confusion. *Maria Nephele* is Elytis's first poem that takes place in an urban setting. The poet must plan a new course of direction if he is to survive among the enraged brontosaurs and "invent a new language" — even if this language is nothing more than a primitive, incomprehensible cry. Maria Nephele is pragmatic; she knows that "weapons are needed to speak for our chaotic times." She feels sympathy for the "dear Poets / who for years feign the invincible souls" and end up as "unclaimed articles . . . the voluntary experimental animals of the Divine." The world rejects the poet as an intellectual removed from reality. For Maria Nephele, though, he is the Homeric Nephelegeretes (the Cloud-Gathering Zeus), the captive of her dreams.

The poet feels tender love "in two dimensions" toward Maria Nephele, who "has come like the light / of a star that vanished / centuries ago." Love enables the poet to overcome the complexity of modern life; it sustains him through hard times of unpopularity and offers to him the magic that destroys "the hard rock." He becomes the "St. John of loves" and descends "from Love ready to establish a white seashore." His purity of feeling unites with the sun, the sea, the winds, and the humble wildflowers and birds that are elevated to spiritual, divine beings. By means of the most minute details, the poet gradually unfolds the web of his poetic vision. The particular in his poetry acquires the dimensions of the universal; he knows how to reveal the hidden dimensions of reality, how to "cross over to the other side," transmit "the divine message / the ambrosia-scented music," and capture from the natural and spiritual world what is "complete and Imperishable." Within the harmonious relationships of nature and life, Elytis discovers a world where Paradise has not been irrevocably lost. "It is a Paradise made of the same material of which Hell is made . . . My innate tendency to sanctify the senses flows directly into the vision of Paradise," says Elytis, contrasting the faith and hope of his poetic voice with the pessimistic cries of our time and the belief that despair and grief have "settled permanently within us."

Maria Nephele is divided into three parts, separated by two interludes. There is also a dialogical prologue, and an epigrammatic epilogue with seven three-line stanzas. Each of the three parts contains seven pairs of poems; the numerical designation of each poem of part I is interrelated with the poems that have corresponding numbers in the other two parts. Pairs of poems in each of the three sections of the work share similar numerical or thematic significance. For instance, "The Forest of Man" and "The Fix" in part I relate to "Pax San Tropezana" and "The Planet Earth" in part II and to "Good Morning, Grief" and "Morning Gymnastics" in part III. And the three pairs of poems designated by number four — "Speech on Beauty" and "The Waterdrop"; "Eau de Verveine" and "Speech on Innocence"; and "Speech on Justice" and "Study of a Nude" — deal with the themes of beauty, purity, justice, innocence, and the glorification of the naked body. Poems designated by the number seven — "The Trojan War" and "Helen"; "The Holy Inquisition" and "St. Francis of Assisi"; and "Stalin" and "The Hungarian Uprising" — refer to significant periods or events that have left their marks on human history — ancient, medieval, modern — and focus on a mythological or historical person. The poems two personae respond freely to each other in lyric, dramatic, or satiric tones that express their aesthetic, philosophical, historical, objective, or subjective views. Placed opposite each other, their monologues converge and are antithetical, analogous, or parallel, according to the manner in which each perceives the other and the world. They exchange place and time: Maria Nephele speaks first in the first and third sections of the work; the Antiphonist does so in the second. The antiphonal composition of the poems is reminiscent of the strophic and antistrophic structure of the choral odes of ancient tragedy and the antiphonal voices in a divine liturgy. Each poem ends with an epigrammatic statement, an oracular response that stands apart. These statements are pointed, ambivalent, paradoxical, ironic, or satiric; they heighten the meaning of each poem, through their sibylline concision revealing the freshness and the brilliant crystallization of the poet's wisdom: "From your thought the sun congeals / in the pomegranate and rejoices."

The mathematical structure of *Maria Nephele* is in accord with "the tendency toward the forces that transcend man, the inevitability of the magical influence of numbers," as in the Pythagorean mystical harmony of numbers. This is the force that binds the physical form of the poem to its intellectual content. The composition of poetic material according to the principle of the harmony of contraries allows Elytis to express complex relationships and principles in a translucent, plastic manner. The poem's main themes revolve around a series of dual antitheses that enable the poet to contrast his feeling for life with the harsh realities of present-day chaos. From the interaction of antithetical forces and images — light and darkness, life and death, height and depth, good and evil, justice and injustice, systole and diastole of time, to mention only a few — Elytis composes a poetic mythology that climaxes in the affirmation of life. His poetic landscape is in continuous transformation: The horizontal, vertical, and diagonal elements in his architectural design are balanced yet in eternal motion, forming a polyhedric metaphor in and of themselves. Elytis introduces form and imposes limitations on himself and his material so that he may work from within. Thus *Maria Nephele* represents the very essence of Elytis's dialectic. Through the voices of Maria Nephele and the Antiphonist, the poet continually raises questions, challenges, and is challenged. The dialogic and dialectical form of the poem is, in the Platonic meaning of these terms, nothing other than the poet's dialogue with himself, as revealed to him through the prism of the feminine soul.

The language of *Maria Nephele* is rich in its multiplicity of meanings and its varied mood, in its depth of feeling and the clarity of its intellectual content, and Elytis makes use of Homeric, Heraclitean, Platonic, and New Testament Greek. (The linguistic and literary allusions in the poem are numerous.) For the first time, Elytis makes departures from the lofty style that marks his earlier books and employs colloquial, familiar expressions that give the poem the immediacy, warmth, and vitality of everyday dialogue. There are also quotations from other languages: Latin, French, German, Italian, and Spanish. *Maria Nephele*'s language reflects the multicolored mosaic of contemporary life, both the sophisticated, highly literary aspects of international culture and the prosaic language of television commercials and advertisements in periodicals with worldwide circulation. The mystifying power of language is as important here as life itself. The metrical patterns of *Maria Nephele* are variable. Although the work is primarily written in flowing free verse, several poems are composed in traditional metrical forms. Others ("Nephele," "Maria Nephele's Song," "Each Moon Confesses," "The Poet's Song," "Morning Gymnastics," and "Ich Sehe Dich") contain intricate rhyme schemes that make them impossible to render accurately in English translation. Elytis has employed alliteration and rhymed couplets in several of his poems, as well as internal rhymes and half-rhymes where they are consistent with the mood and content of the individual poem.

In *Maria Nephele* one may also discover many references to art, music, poetry, philosophies, and aesthetic movements of all times and places; to the differences between ancient Greek art, Renaissance art, and contemporary art — Minoan frescoes, Etruscan painting, and the works of El Greco, Piero della Francesca, Rublev, Klee, Mondrian, de Chirico; to ancient poets and philosophers — Homer, Sappho, Archilochus, Heraclitus, Plato, St. John of the Apocalypse, St. Augustine; and to more recent poets and philosophers — Góngora y Argote, Apollinaire, Hölderlin, Novalis, Alberti, Breton, Fourier, Ungaretti, Solomos, Empeirikos. Such allusions point to the universal scope of the poet's work and his affinity with other artists, philosophers, and poets, since "the common trait that characterizes the race of the poets is their contention with everyday reality."

In awarding Odysseus Elytis the Nobel Prize in literature for 1979, the Swedish Academy cited his "poetry which, against the background of Greek tradition, depicts with sensuous strength and intellectual clear-sightedness modern man's struggle for freedom and creativity." The poems in *Maria Nephele* are firmly rooted not only in the Greek tradition but also in the European. Together with Solomos, Cavafy, Seferis, and Ritsos, Elytis proves that modern Greek poetry, with its glorious and uninterrupted tradition of nearly three millennia, does not exist in isolation. It lies within the mainstream of the development of international ideological and aesthetic movements. *Maria Nephele* shows Elytis driven by a heightened awareness and experimenting with a new kind of poetics — newly complex, more intricately woven around dialectic, aesthetic, and intellecual antitheses. Myth, memory, and history are haunted by tradition and continuity. With the fusion of traditional and modern poetic sensibilities, Elytis has fashioned a poetic logos that is universal and archetypal. The duality of the poem's structure directs us to both its spiritual and secular nature. "I personally believe," Elytis states, "that a virgin eye that has just returned from the rounds of our familiar things has more to tell us than a common eye that had the privilege of wandering in virgin lands." Elytis probes into man's existence in the twentieth century, and especially the decades of the sixties and the seventies, and through dream and fantasy he extracts the distilled essence of life, in accord with his belief that "the lack of fantasy transforms man into an invalid of reality."

Elytis has remarked that he considers poetry "a source of innocence full of revolutionary forces. It is my mission to direct these forces against a world my conscience cannot accept, precisely so as to bring that world through continuous metamorphoses more in harmony with my dreams . . . In the hope of obtaining a freedom from all constraints and the justice which could be identified with absolute light, I am an idolator who, without wanting to do so, arrives at Christian sainthood." *Maria Nephele* is the embodiment of the poet's incessant search for those eternal values that constitute the very fabric of life. The poet becomes once more the hierophant of man's noblest and profoundest aspirations. Elytis has described poetry as a continuous war against time and decay; as the gift of God: "That's why I write. Because poetry begins there where death does not have the last word. It is the end of one life and the beginning of another which is the same as the first one but reaches very deeply, to the farthest point the soul has been able to explore, to the boundaries of the contraries where the Sun and Hades touch each other. The endless course toward the natural light, which is the Logos, and the Uncreated light, which is God." Rich with some of the finest lyricism in contemporary poetry, *Maria Nephele* is Elytis's testament in defense of man's dignity and his inviolable spirit.

Athan Anagnostopoulos

But I say unto you, That ye resist not evil.

— Matthew 5:39

Divine, toil, feel: On the other side I am the same.

— Elytis

MARIA NEPHELE

THE PRESENCE

M.N. I walk among the thorns, among the dark places,
toward what is going to happen and to the past,
and I have for my only weapon, my only defense,
my fingernails purple like the cyclamen.

A. I saw her everywhere. Holding a glass and gazing into the void. Listening to records lying on the floor. Walking in the street in bell-bottom trousers and an old raincoat. In front of the windows of children's stores. Sadder then. And in discotheques, more nervous, biting her nails. She smokes countless cigarettes. She's pale and beautiful. But if you speak to her she doesn't listen at all. As if something is happening elsewhere — something she alone hears and is terrified by. She holds your hand tightly, sheds tears, but she is not *there*. I never touched her and never took anything from her.

M.N. He understood nothing. All the time he kept saying to me, "Do you remember?" Remember what? Only dreams I remember, because I see them at night. But in the daylight I feel bad — how shall I say it? — unprepared. I found myself in life so suddenly — where I least expected it. I said, "Bah, I'll get used to it." And everything around me kept running. Things and men kept running, running — until I too started running like crazy. But it seems I overdid it. Because — I don't know — something strange happened in the end. First I saw the dead man and then the murder occurred. First came the blood and then the blow and the cry. And now when I hear the rain I don't know what's in store for me . . .

A. "Why don't they bury people standing, like the Bishops?" — that's what she said to me. And once, I remember, summertime on the island, when all of us were returning from a sleepless night, at daybreak, we jumped over the railings at the garden of the Museum. She was dancing on the stones and didn't see a thing.

M.N. I saw his eyes. I saw old olive groves.

A. I saw a grave stele. A maiden in relief
on the stone. She seemed sad and held in her palm
a little bird.

M.N. He was looking at me, I know it, he was looking at me. We were both looking at the same stone. We were looking at each other through the stone.

A. She was calm and held in her palm a little bird.

M.N. She was sitting. And she was dead.

A. She was sitting and held in her palm a little bird. You will never hold a bird — you are not worthy!

M.N. O, if only they let me, if only they let me.

A. Who should let you?

M.N. He who allows nothing.

A. He, he who allows nothing
tears himself from his shadow and walks somewhere else.

M.N. His words are white and ineffable
and his eyes are deep and sleepless . . .

A. But he had taken the whole upper part of the stone. And along with it, her name, too.

M.N. ΑΡΙΜΝΑ . . . It's as if I still see the letters carved into the light . . . ΑΡΙΜΝΑ ΕΦΗ ΕΛ . . .

A. It was missing. The whole upper part was missing. There were no letters at all.

M.N. ΑΡΙΜΝΑ ΕΦΗ ΕΛ . . . there, on this ΕΛ, the stone was cut and broken. I remember this well.

A. She must have seen this too in her dream; that's why she remembers it.

M.N. In my dream, yes. In a great sleep which will come sometime, full of light and warmth and little stone stairsteps.
Embracing, the children will pass in the streets just as in old

Italian movies. From everywhere you'll hear songs and see huge women on small balconies watering their flowers.

A. A big sea balloon will take us high then, now here, now there, the wind will blow toward us. First the silver domes will stand out, and then the belfries. The streets will appear narrower, straighter than we imagined them. The rooftops with the snow-white antennae for television sets. And the hills all around, and the kites — glancingly we'll pass beside them. Until at a certain moment we'll view the whole sea. The souls above it will let out small white puffs of steam.

M.N. I've raised my hands directly against the black mountains and the evil spirits of this world. I've asked love "why" and rolled her on the floor. Wars occurred and recurred, and not even a rag was left to hide deep within our things and forget it. Who listens? Who ever listened? Judges, priests, gendarmes, which is your country? A body is left to me and I offer it. On it they cultivate, those who know, the sacred things, as the gardeners in Holland the tulips. And in it are drowned all those who never learned about the sea and swimming . . .
Flowing of the sea and you, far-off influence of the stars — stand by me!

A. I've raised my hand directly against the
unexorcised evil spirits of the world,
and from the sickly place I returned
to the sun and the light self-exiled!

M.N. And from the many tempests I returned
among the people self-exiled!

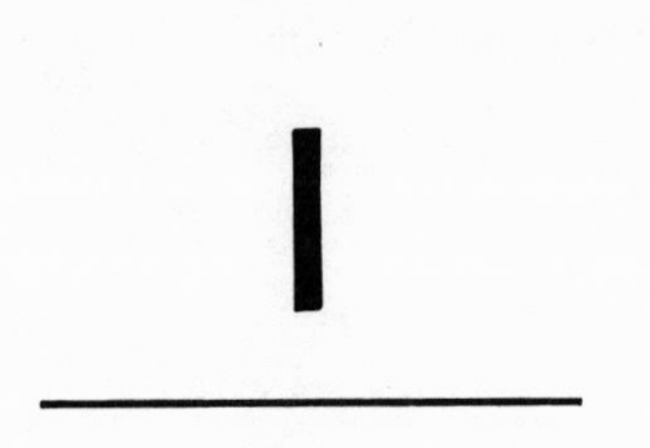

Maria Nephele says:

THE FOREST OF MEN

Flowing of the sea and you,
far-off influence of the stars — stand by me!
From the waters of the night sky look
how I rise
curved
like the new Moon
and dripping blood.

Poet, my neglected cicada,
no one has noonday anymore;
snuff out Attica and come to me.
I'll take you to the forest of men
and I'll dance for you naked with tom-tom and masks
and offer myself to you amid roarings and howlings.
I'll show you the man Baobab
and the man Phagus Carnamenti
the old woman Cimmulius and her whole clan
worm-eaten by the parasites;
I'll show you the man Bumbacarao Uncarabo
his wife Ibou-Ibou
and their deformed children,
the mushroom dogs
Cingua Banga and Iguana Brescus.
Don't be afraid
with my hand out in front like a storm lantern
I'll lead you
and rush upon you;
my fingernails will tear into your flesh
truth — don't they say so? — is painful
and needs you to know your blood,
needs your wounds;
through them alone will pass — if ever the life
you vainly sought will pass —
with the wind whistling, and the spirits,
and the maidens with the suns on their bicycles . . .

And the Antiphonist responds:

THE FIX

Whatever you see — you see it well
provided it is: an A n n o u n c e m e n t.
The tiny cloud gliding with a fair wind the Moon
the alligator of the trees
and the sullen tranquillity of the lagoons
with the distant put-put of the outboard motor
if the world were named once and for all: an A n n o u n c e m e n t.

Poetry O my Saint — forgive me
but I need to stay alive
to cross over to the other side;
anything would be preferable
to my slow assassination by the past.
And if upon me every tempest
remains indelible like an encaustic
the fulfillment of my days will come
boustrophedon I'll annihilate myself.

Unless even this does not exist
if in the depths of the oceans
sinking the golden days took with them
once and for all the idol
the Light-Tree
with thousands of blinding flashes of birds
and the Months all around on tiptoe
gathering in their aprons
crocuses small tadpoles of the ethers.

It's because men have not wished it, otherwise . . .
Amid the void I hoarded, and now again
amid my hoardings I remain a void.

O farewell Paradises and unsought gifts,
I leave, I go straight above me
there far away where I belong.

Maria Nephele says:

Come! Emerge! Depart!
Without club and cave,
amid the enraged brontosaurs,
try to adjust by yourself
to invent a new language perhaps shrieking:
e e e e e.

When you'll hear me again and again singing for you,
singing for you in the nights with the xylophone:
"Into the forest I went dragoo-droogoo
the trees devoured me droogoo-droo
tore me to pieces dragoo-droogoo
threw me to the birds of prey droogoo-droo."

The Law that I am
will not subdue me.

And the Antiphonist responds:

The moment has come. Maria Nephele
take my hand — I follow you;
and the other I raise — look — with the palm
turned inward spreading the fingers,
a heavenly flower:
"Hubris" as we'd say, or even "Star."

Hubris-Star Hubris-Star
that's the fix, friends
we must keep in touch.
Don't laugh at my great ineptness
you know that the weather is adverse.

Demonstrate such well-aimed ineptness
and look: the God!

Maria Nephele says:

NEPHELE

I live day by day — who knows what tomorrow will bring.
My one hand crumples the money and the other smoothes it over

You see, weapons are needed to speak for our chaotic times
and we must keep in line too with the so-called "national ideals"

Why stare at me, scribe, you who never put on a soldier's uniform,
the art of making money is a military trait, too

You may spend sleepless nights — writing thousands of sad lines
or covering the walls with revolutionary slogans

Other people will always see you as an intellectual,
and only I, who love you: as a captive of my dreams.

So that if love is indeed, as they say, the "common denominator"
I must be Maria Nephele and you, alas, Nephelegeretes.

Inscribe yourself somewhere in whichever way and
afterward efface yourself with magnanimity.

And the Antiphonist responds:

NEPHELEGERETES

Ah how beautiful to be a Nephelegeretes
to write epic poems like Homer and not care
not bother whether you're liked or not
nothing

Undisturbed you enjoy antipopularity
thus; with magnanimity; as though you own
a mint and shut it down
you dismiss all the personnel
and sustain a poverty that nobody else has
entirely your own.
The hour when in their offices desperately
hanging on their telephones
the boors struggle for a nothing
you ascend inside Love
smeared all over with soot but agile
like a chimney sweep
you descend from Love ready to establish
a white seashore of your own

no downpayment

you undress as those who understand the stars undress
and with sweeping strokes you head for the open sea to weep
freely . . .

It is bigamy to love and to dream.

Maria Nephele says:

PATMOS

It is before you know it that death brings changes;
by living with its fingerprints upon us,
half-savages with hair disheveled, we bend
gesturing over incomprehensible harps. But
the world departs . . .
Hey, hey, the beautiful cannot occur twice,
love cannot occur.

Pity pity world
the future dead dominate you;
and no one no one ever chanced
ever chanced to hear yet
even the voice of angels even gushing waters
even that "Come!" which in nights of great sleeplessness I dreamed

There there I'd go to a rocky island
which the sun treads slantwise like a crab
and the whole sea trembling listens and replies.

In panoply with sixteen pieces of luggage sleeping bags and maps
plastic bags close-up and telephoto lenses
crates with bottles of mineral water
I set out — for the second time — but nothing.

Already nine o'clock at the quay on Mykonos
I fainted amid ouzos and English words
habituée of a light sky where all
things weigh twice their weight
as the umbilical cord is stretched by the stars
to be cut and you perish . . .

I slept as one could only sleep
in a bed warmed by the backs of others;
I felt I was walking on a deserted seashore

And the Antiphonist responds:

THE APOCALYPSE

Narrow the road — the wide one I have never known
unless it was only once
when I was kissing you and listening to the sea . . .

And it's from that time I say — it's the same sea
reaching in my sleep that ate away the hard rock
and opened the vast dimensions. Words I learned
like the passages of fish green
with blue chalk branded
ravings when awake I unlearned
and again swimming I felt and interpreted
St. John of loves
with my face down
on the blankets of a bed in a provincial hotel
with the bulb bare at the end of the cord
and the black cockroach motionless over the wash basin.
Why why would one be a man
the degree of luxury in the kingdom of life
what may it mean
unless you have ears to hear
don't fear what you are destined to suffer.

I did not fear
I not at all humbly though I endured
I saw death three times
I was thrown out of the doors.

If you have ears to hear. I heard
a din as if from a sea conch
and turning toward the light I suddenly saw
four boys with dark-skinned faces
who were blowing and pushing, pushing and carrying
a thin strip of land surrounded by a stone wall
all in all seven olive trees

Maria Nephele says:

where the moon was bleeding and you heard only
the wind's footsteps on the rotten wood.
Knee-deep in the water I began to shine
from within me a strange yearning
I spread my legs
slowly very slowly my bowels began
purple dark blue orange to fall;
bending down with affection I washed them carefully
one by one especially at the points where I saw
scars left by the tooth marks of the Invisible.

Then I gathered them all in my apron
without walking I kept advancing
music was blowing and pushing me
patches of sea here — patches of sea farther down.
My God where does one go when one has no destiny
where does one go when one has no star
empty the sky empty the body
and only sadness round full
inside the half-moon stirring its thorns
one more you can't ever catch
female sea urchin.

At this I awoke in the strange house;
groping in the dark my hand
found the sharp point of the small scissors.
Solution of the skin's continuity
the sharp point solution of the world's continuity.
This side ruin — the other side salvation.
This side the mercurochrome, the tensoplast,
the other side the wild beast devastating the wilderness,
howling biting
dragging the sun through thick smoke.

When you hear wind
it is the Calm that has turned into a vampire.

And the Antiphonist responds:

and amid them an old man looking like a shepherd
his feet bare upon the rock.

"I am," he said. "Do not fear
what you are destined to suffer."
And stretching his right hand
he showed me the seven deep furrows on his palm:
"These are the great sorrows
and they will be inscribed on your face,
but I will erase them with this very same hand
that brings them."

And suddenly behind his hand I saw — there appeared
a mob of many men stupefied with terror
who shouted and ran, ran and screamed
"Here comes Abaddon, here comes the Destroyer."
I felt great turmoil and anger
overcame me. But he continued:
"Let the evil-doer do more evil. And let the filthy man
become filthier. And let the just man
become more just." And because I sighed
with boundless calm he passed his hand
slowly over my face
and it was sweet like honey yet my bowels became sour.
"Again you must utter prophecies over peoples and nations
and languages and many kings,"
he said; and emitting white flames he united with the sun.

Such was my first dream that still
I cannot separate it from the voices of the sea
and cannot keep it pure.
A dream cannot exist in words.
My lie is so true
that my lips still burn.

If you will not keep one foot outside
the Earth you will never be able to stand on it.

Maria Nephele says:

SPEECH ON BEAUTY

Be fearful
if you wish to awaken in yourself the instinct of the Beautiful;

or if not then since we live in the century of photography
immobilize it: whatever next to us
continually acts with incredible gestures:
the Inconceivable!

a) a woman's two beautiful hands (or even a man's) that would have grown used to the wild doves
b) a wire whose memories would be
all electric current and unsuspecting birds
c) a cry that could be considered eternally timely
d) the irrational phenomenon of the open sea.

You must have understood of course what I mean.

We are the negative of dream,
that's why we appear black and white
and live decay
in a minute reality. But
Das Reine Ladies and Gentlemen
kann sich nur darstellen im Unreinen
und versuchst Du das Edle zu geben
ohne Gemeines
so wird es als das Allerunnatürlichste
says He who succeeded in treading
the Upper Paths.

And he must have known something.

My God what blueness You spend so that we will not see You!

And the Antiphonist responds:

THE WATERDROP

My lips burn and grief glows
a drop of pure water over the abyss
dark filled with weeds; only the soul
lit up like an old church
                                        shows that we'll die in spring . . .

Ding-ding the chamomile: I got tired of waiting
ding-ding the mallow flower: I got bored with worrying
ding-ding: man has been such
from the beginning
                                  and I didn't even know it!

Those footsteps on the dry leaves
groaning the bull of Time

The Pelasgian stone masonry in all the length of my life
I walk alongside it
until the dark sea appears
and over it will flare like Bengal lights my three stars!

All things a waterdrop
of beauty trembling on the lashes;
a grief diaphanous like Athos hanging from the sky
with boundless visibility
where all things generate degenerate
Charon falls to his knees and rises again stronger
and falls again strengthless sinking into the abyss.

All alone the waterdrop powerful over the abyss.

In the village of my language Grief is called the Radiant Lady.

Maria Nephele says:

THROUGH THE MIRROR

Through fishing comes the sea
and it is in its smell that the fish flash
don't search in vain

Somewhere between Tuesday and Wednesday
your true day must have been overlooked.

Supra-essential you go on while over your head
spread the depths with their colorful pebbles like stars.

O music O cloudy Sunday
in a distant suburb with two-story houses closed up
under the surface of the water where I bend
as over a mirror and stare at myself
for many hours how to pass through,
pass over to
the other side of things
with my curly hair uncurling
circles one after another
and climb down all seven heavens until

the reflection
of the angels seizes me
Yiannis Anna Nikos with enormous
wings like Theotokopoulos'
and in midair they'll start softly
a psalmody until the windows will open again,
the florists will communicate with huge anemones
placed over their ears like earphones;

Signals — mysterious words
"Asterobadon" "Idiolathes" "Mikyon" — which means
your will is done and the voice of the earth
is already confirmed in the flowers. At any moment it will appear

And the Antiphonist responds:

AEGEÏS

I don't know where; it's not in dream
it's not in old times perhaps not on this earth
but even if it were
                                        three scales higher
than what is possible for man's black finger to conjure up,
the land in which no one dwells anymore
continues to exist.

In our ignorance there
Justice
formulated in the language of birds
is reproduced continually overflowing the city walls
sparkling from one conscience to another
empty of body like a Hertzian
wave not finding an antenna to receive it and yet
transmitting the divine message
the ambrosia-scented music

and this is completed
in all the sound combinations from the hanging waters
falling until dawn "by force,"
as we'd say, exist there
made of jasper and fine copper
cobalt blue terra cotta and ocher all the works of art
which man could with unimaginable
toil detach from the Complete and Imperishable but impossible.

          Perhaps had I not
once ascended even myself
those flights of steps of the undying summer
a high mountainous sea,
had I not for the sake of King Evenor
put on the dark blue mantle
to judge others and be judged by them
in the vertical hour of midnight . . .

Maria Nephele says:

in the very same complete world of antimatter
as scientists tell us — and which is feeling
made tangible
a concert that deigned to be turned into a garden.

And I who was created to pursue the miracle
on an impressive hill like the Escorial
now what do I discover?
The martyrdom of St. Maurice
who lived again in our times in a different cloth
over and over thousands of times.
The eminent officials with their golden epaulets
and their black instruments
in stinking well-barred cellars over and over.
The writer who hides his manuscripts — where? — from whom? —
who is he — what is this we call superior
power by the grace of God or the grace of tanks
O
music O cloudy Sunday
in the inside world of the mirror where I pace
searching for my true day;
where I hold and open the sea like an old umbrella
over my head
the depths shine with their colorful pebbles like stars.

Children and grandchildren of negation
are all of them bastards.

And the Antiphonist responds:

They live still live in me
once and for all seen
from above the fields grooved straight as Mondrian's paintings,

the churchyards with the girls stark naked
holding myrtle

and the drum the drum
"sun-water" "sun-water"
while the laws of gravity were finally slackening
the mind pulled up the birds and the whole thick forest of heaven
  to the heights.

This.
    And now only
what is preserved in superstitions,
what from the shadeless proto-earth
we exorcise in the nights standing directly facing
the turbulent sea disembarked seafarers
who lost the divine wreckage forever.

Brought to a mathematical clarity superstitions would help us
  to perceive the deeper structure of the world.

Maria Nephele says:

THUNDERBOLT STEERS

What's this that gets entangled in my hair
like the bat and I shake my head in terror;
sometimes like an invisible net cast from afar
it pulls me and I cannot escape from it;
it seizes my mind as I hear traps seize birds
I stop thinking and it sets me free;
I run to the mirrors and I see nothing.

Death is elsewhere.

Thunderbolt steers.

You men will perish
the comb in your hand will stop still one morning in the air
and the mirror will show the subcutaneous web
of tissues where time
has been trapped like an insect in despair.

Death is elsewhere.

Don't let me run for I'll perish.
The grace to weep has not been granted me but I fear.
I have no relatives
                    in all my life
I've tried hard to create a youth made of stone.

I've filled love with crosses.

Grief beautifies
                    because we resemble it.

And the Antiphonist responds:

HYMN TO MARIA NEPHELE

Now I'll stretch out my open arms
and inside the currents which I'll create
without coming near you'll appear
Iris Maria Nephele
green in the big novelty stores
violet in the underground cafés
red in the funerals of the poor
and blue in the sleep of infants;

Iris Maria Nephele
with your nightgown in the wind
flying and asleep
as in a painting by Léonor Fini
chrysalis of my sleep.

Tra un fiore colto e l'altro donato
l'inesprimibile nulla.

You are beautiful like a natural phenomenon
in what within you leads to the eel and the wildcat;
you are the rainfall between the apartment houses;
the god-sent interruption of the electric current;
astrology will observe your bed
and will base its prognostics on your despair;
you are beautiful like despair
like the paintings the bourgeois detest
and will buy in the future with billions
Iris Maria Nephele
with the charm of your buttocks
sitting down suddenly unsuspectingly on a blade.

The terrorist
is the boorish man of miracles.

Maria Nephele says:

THE TROJAN WAR

If we lived on the reverse side at least
would we see everything right? Bah. Reversal
has an obstinate permanence;
it constitutes as we say the rule.
Which means that if we manage to live,
certainly we live by exceptions.
We pretend that nothing happens
exactly so that in the end something will happen
outside and above derision.
A cherry the hour when all miseries
are wintering inside it
and it despite them pure omnipotent
blameless glows showing
what man's superiority could have been.

The drop of blood each April
free for everyone.

Unlucky front guards and backward
drivers of the heavy tanks of the sky
even the clouds are laid with mines
beware: spring depends on us.

Let's give the earth back to our feet.
The green to the green, the Neanderthal
to the Neanderthal. Muscles are no use anymore
there's need for bestial love
there's need for a tigress' leap into ideas.
As long as there are Achaeans there will be a fair Helen
even though the hand is in one place and the neck in another.

Each era with its Trojan War.

Far off in the farthest reaches of the Lamb
the war continues.

And the Antiphonist responds:

HELEN

Maria Nephele undoubtedly
is a sharp girl
a real threat to the future;
sometimes she gleams like a knife
and a drop of blood on her
has the same significance
the Lambda of the *Iliad* once had.

Maria Nephele goes forward
redeemed from the abhorrent meaning of the eternal cycle.

By her mere existence
she finishes off half of mankind.

Maria Nephele lives at the antipodes of Ethics
she is full of ethos.

When she says "I'll sleep with this man"
she means that she'll kill History once again.
One should see then what enthusiasm seizes the birds.

On the other hand in her way
she perpetuates the nature of the olive tree.
According to the moment she becomes
now silvery now dark blue.

That's why adversaries keep
marching to war — look:
some with their social theories
many others merely brandishing flowers.

Each era with its Helen.

From your thought the sun congeals
in the pomegranate and rejoices.

MARIA NEPHELE'S SONG

"Pity the girl" they say
shaking their heads
as if they mourn for me
why do they nag me!

In the clouds I ramble
like lovely lightning
and what I give or take
turns into rain.

Here boys look at me
I cut with a double edge;
in the morning when I sulk
I swear at Virgins

and at night when I tumble
over the grass of every man
as in a spear fight
droogoo-droogoo-droo.

Joy I have not known
and I trample on grief;
Like an angel I roam
over the abyss.

II

The Antiphonist says:

PAX SAN TROPEZANA

What a buffalo cow the earth has turned into nowadays!
She plods on all fours and snorts with joy
onward ho!
Thanks to the ruling fathers
peace reigns
living things both small and great there ships move about . . .

Painted breasts two-tone pants
super-sized straw hats of all sorts
coats-of-arms of rich princes aspirant masochists
writers-at-a-distance
actors for twenty-four hours
they piss into the sea and emit small cries
pseudo-European style:
oh-oh oh-oh

High in the sky black voids
gape and the osmosis
of the souls spills over, a thick-flowing smoke.
Sometimes a Saint's glance can be made out
fierce as never before
"it's meaningless — the meaning is elsewhere"
colorful fumbling multitudes keep on
with half-closed eyes crawling
onward ho!
Pax
Pax San Tropezana
peace reigns.
Pseudo-European style all things are said
generate degenerate
on easy terms in installments.
Time of spare parts:
blow a tire — change a tire
you lose a Jimmy — you find a Bob.

And Maria Nephele responds:

THE PLANET EARTH

Ah this is not a planet
filled with chickens and sheep
and other silly stooping creatures.
At the very edge of the Universe this neglected planet
with its very tiny small oceans
and its little Himalayas,
with its four billion wingless two-legged beings
eternally fighting for altars and hearths
oil wells and other wealth-producing regions.
This is not a planet
packed with poisonous gases
exposed to the rains of meteorites,
to thoughts of philosophers,
to long struggles for freedom
(our own always — never other people's).
A chess game for crows well trained
always to profit from both sides
"Black birds" as they say "black messages."

No no this is not a planet
rather it's a fallacy leading too far back
to Zeus Christ Buddha Mohammed
who at long last have
languished so that all of us
merely because of acquired speed
would remain in the position of an obeisant man.
The counting down to perfect total extinction.

The only thing that will remain unchanged
is vengeance.
Iron and stone have their own way
of overcoming us
and we'll enter a new stone age
we'll be terrified amid the enraged brontosaurs;

The Antiphonist says:

C'est très pratique, as Annette used to say,
the beautiful waitress of the Tahiti.
Nineteen lovers had signed her breasts
along with their place of origin
a small tender geography.

Yet I think that in essence she was a homosexual.

Eat progress
both its rinds and its pits.

And Maria Nephele responds:

then perhaps we'll be nostalgic
for the precision and perfection
of a Patek Philippe.

Hey you Gentlemen of Technocracy
move to the right a bit, please:
reserve a seat for me in Alpha Centauri
and then we'll see.

Unfortunately even the Earth
rotates at our own expense.

The Antiphonist says:

THE DAGGER

Deep in sleep are the blasphemers and look: our moon
took heart to appear. The mountain uttered again
sacred incomprehensible gravities
from leaf to leaf,
the water's fawn and the caper.
On their sides motionless and asleep
the horses very tall,
and down below very far, half the valley in white.
Courage. Now. It's the moment
to emerge, my God, from obscurity.
In bathtubs with smooth tiles beautiful women
reclining in water vapors
mark the deviation: the planet departs.
The husk will appear riddled with black
holes and flashes of lightning and slowly
man will turn inward
until he vanishes entirely.
Courage. Now.
That I may rescue pleasure at least my God.
Give me the dagger.

It is rude
to offer Charon hand-kissing.

And Maria Nephele responds:

EACH MOON CONFESSES

Each moon confesses and hides among the trees
    lest you perceive it;
you've mixed up the seasons so that not even you yourself
    know from whence the message will be received.

You're one of those men to whom they gave a big piece of paper
    to write and didn't deign to touch his pen;
to whom luck came like a dimple on the cheek and who never
    thought to smile.

You're the man over whom they cast the net in his bath to
    kill him yet who still rules his kingdom;
who pushes love out the window and then laments
    and says the laws wrong him.

Each moon confesses and you pretend you don't
    understand.
You know you wear the sun — and that before the moon sets
    you ascend.

Give your time freely
        if you wish a little dignity left to you.

The Antiphonist says:

THE ANCESTRAL PARADISE

I don't know a thing about original sin
and other concoctions of Western man.
Yet truly there far away
in the freshness of the first days
before our mother's hovel
how beautiful it was!

The white garments of the angels I think I remember,
they closed in front but they left them unbuttoned
exactly like girls with their robes, girls who work at beauty parlors
a marvel — and all the geraniums
on a long whitewashed stone wall
turned toward the wind, you watched them grinding
endlessly the sun's black sap.

Fresh days in umber and sienna
when the island seemed like a boundless Lasithi
weightless and gently placed
over a dazzling shattered sea.

One leg upon the other
on the sandy shore rippled by the wind
full of golden dust from the spurs
galloping I saw I remember
girls of the sirocco with tender buttocks
unfolding heads of clover hair;
and my heart opposite the bare mountains
thump-thump echoed like a motor caïque.

It was in the time of the Shining Leaf
when Sathes and Merione reigned.

In the nights I had meaning — I offered it to all the nightingales
and my sweet sleep was filled with half-moons
tiny brooks in Do major and viola d'amore.

And Maria Nephele responds:

THE KITE

And yet I was made to be a kite.
I liked the heights even when
I lay face down on my pillow
punished
for hours and hours.
I felt my room was ascending
I wasn't dreaming — it was ascending
I was afraid and I liked it.
It was what I saw — how shall I call it? —
something like the "memory of the future"
full of trees that left mountains that changed face,
geometric fields with curly thickets
like pudenda — I was afraid yet I liked
to touch the belfries lightly,
caress the bells like testicles and vanish . . .

Men with light umbrellas passed by sidelong
and smiled at me;
sometimes they knocked at my windowpane: "Young lady!"
I was afraid and I liked it.
They were men "on top" as I called them,
not men "on the bottom";
they had long beards and many held gardenias in their hands;
some of them opened the balcony door halfway
and put weird records on my record player.
I remember "Annetta with Sandals"
"Geyzer of Spietsburg"
the "No fruit we bit no May will come to us"
(yes, I remember others too)
I repeat — I was not dreaming
and suddenly "Open your dress halfway, I have a bird for you."
It was brought to me by that Knight-bicyclist
one day when I was sitting pretending to read,
he was leaning his bicycle very carefully against my bed;
then he pulled the string and I billowed into the air

The Antiphonist says:

There were daisies you could eat
and others that kindled in the dark like fireworks;
the broom shrubs groaned and made love;
under your feet passed stars
like schools of fish, and the dark blue
straits proceeded into your bowels —
how beautiful it was!

The angels teased me; many times
gathered around me they asked:
"What is pain?" and "What is sickness?" and didn't really know.
I didn't know I hadn't ever heard about
the Tree through which death entered the world.
Well? Was death the truth? Not this — the other one
that will come with the first cry of the newborn child? Was injustice
the truth? The rage of nations? And the toil day and night?

In the bed of herbs I suckled vervain
and all the archangels Michael Gabriel
Uriel Raphael
Gabael Achar Ariukh
Belial Zabulon burst into laughter shaking
their golden heads like ears of corn;
knowing that the only death the only one is the one
men created in their minds

And their great lie the Tree did not exist.

One "makes up" truth
just as he makes up falsehood.

And Maria Nephele responds:

my colorful underwear gleamed
I watched how translucent those who love become
tropical fruits and handkerchiefs from a distant continent;
I was afraid and I liked it
my room was ascending
or I — I never understood.
I am porcelain and magnolia,
my hand derives from the ancient Incas
I slip through doors like
an infinitely small earthquake
felt only by dogs and infants;
I must necessarily be a monster
and yet adversity
has always nourished me, and this is due
to those with the pointed hats
who talk secretly with my mother
in the nights to decide about it. Sometimes
the bugle's sound from the distant barracks
unraveled me like a streamer and everyone around me
applauded — fragments of incredible years
all in midair.
In the bath nearby the faucets running
with my face down against my pillow
I gazed at the fountains as immaculate white sprayed me;
how beautiful my God how beautiful
trampled on the ground
still holding before my eyes
such a distant mourning of the past.

Fantasy is worn inside out
and in all sizes.

The Antiphonist says:

EAU DE VERVEINE

I said: I am pure
washed with distillation of vervain
90 proof by birth
a Greek among savages.

"Without sighs or fear."

I'll detach my white sign
and direct it
with the speed of a soul
toward the invisible peak.

The infinite exists for us
as the tongue for a deaf-mute.

And Maria Nephele responds:

SPEECH ON INNOCENCE

And I add: your shadow
is a bad counselor;
walk always
beneath the culminating sun.

"Without limits without terms."

Because Ladies and Gentlemen
what the swallows impute to us
— the spring we didn't bring —
is precisely our innocence.

Keep Privacy within the Unblushing.

The Antiphonist says:

THE UPPER TARQUINIA

We who live hung up
in the dust of centuries
in a long and tedious Palazzo Pitti
perfect in perspective and proportions
with the white luster at the collar
and the beauty spot on the cheek
we eat sleep circulate
in perfect chiaroscuro
almost beneath the earth;
time for us to knock down the walls
I mean we should open the passageway
in the roof that will allow us
to rise for an instant from within this earth
to the freshness of the tombs!

O Tarquinia the dead who rejoice
in the sun of horses and the air of flutes
will teach us the unbroken continuity

there! at the third height! with the reins of spring
in their fingers, Troiluses and Achilleses
face to face — and between the two
myriads of dark green laurel berries
the speckled words of the Gods

Thus once from a virgin's birthing
long before Maria the winds were unleashed
colorful and the young little chicks the nestlings
of all kinds arrived gently
among the huge blue bellflowers
fearlessly to sit. They are the same ones
that now sway near the trees
with huge rosy ribbons on the branches
as he passes naked with his brick-red body

And Maria Nephele responds:

THE EYE OF THE LOCUST

Ah,
how should I not be afraid of insects!
That are like big bugs that resemble us
like huge men way up to there
with open cupboards that chew and eat
with enormous soles of feet
which easily could crush you whole.

Two or three yards beneath the earth

my own alibi. I won't betray it.
I'll never consent to speak about
the immense rooms with the boards that creaked
each time Saint Simeon stepped on them
enraged and left his three black stones
on the lavatory: one for the outside world
one for the inside; the third for the other the invisible one

Think

truly
I'm not much different from Sophie von Kühn;
I myself like petrifactions,
plaid cloaks flowers
even tuberculosis if there still existed
a way for you to die and be buried princely
armies of the night with ready bayonets
because I still cry secretly
I still delve in dreams
of dark times of the heavens
so much that if at that moment you try to embrace me
you get smeared with stars

In a pit of time

The Antiphonist says:

the Flutist
one foot in front — and the peploi billowing
the souls, the newborn butterflies.

But see what I mean by all this
which we the living, the idiots, between two perils
not even interesting, forget:
the house is not always smaller than the mountain
man is not always bigger than the flower
all the distances are false
that the eye gives us and in vain I believe
we boast saying
"The world is this."

The world is this
the smoke that chases the dog
the plant that rises and runs with the music
the children that paint on the walls
and open their umbrellas exactly like ancient Aeolians
to ascend carrying along the most virgin part
of things. The synthesis
of all this.
A life full to perfection.
Piero della Francesca last angel
of this earth — hold on!

It is in piety that we shall denude ourselves.

The tomorrow of our life will be life again
transferred to the upper Tarquinia.
Go on. Give the signal. We shall never become soldiers.

We must create antibodies even for responsibility.

And Maria Nephele responds:

as you walk there unsuspecting
suddenly you feel the houses around you break
and a smell of grandfather and sulfur
and phosphorus spills over
to grab you by the throat and bind you to earth

Even there heaven gushes forth

something like a very distant daybreak
a sea rolling and white
and always upside-down as though through diopters
I would run microscopic
along the whole length of the black walls of factories
where a blast furnace burns and the statue
of Giorgio de Chirico moves imperceptibly

And I would know

nothing.
A gust of wind all of us and nature doesn't even stir

Nothing!

Well then I've made up my mind:
to isolate some thrill
at random and magnify it three times
mainly out of obstinacy or if not even from a
disposition to see what happens when
you go counter to money to the wind
to security to agony;
always between Lady and Kore
always between Prosperity and Death.

By its very nature darkness
must be a receiver of stolen goods, too.

The Antiphonist says:

HYMN IN TWO DIMENSIONS

Now I love you in two dimensions

like an Etruscan figure
like a mark by Klee that was a fish
you proceed dodecaphonic
nerve-racking
lightninglike
beautiful
with a wave of the Caribbean in the folds of your dress
with the heavy blue beads of Pandrosou Street
around your neck.

Figure watery idol
that has come like the light
of a star that vanished
centuries ago.

Then I hear waters and perceive you.
Although you have no idea
(the Signal Commander never had knowledge of his mission)
and I watch behind the paleness of the make-up
the endless road that I followed
to speak to you like this

Voie lactée ô soeur lumineuse

The only fate that I didn't want
my God — that have I undertaken.

In a bad distribution
God always loses.

And Maria Nephele responds:

LOYALTY OATH

Observe carefully the fragment-
ariness of my everyday life
and its seeming inconsequence.
Where it is aimed
and with what further intentions
it tries to develop
and acquire a deeper meaning.
It seeks to discourage the research of scientists
for the benefit of the authenticity of the human vision.

To this
en las purpureas horas
I make no concession whatsoever.

It's impossible for me to see myself
other
than as an antinarrative synthesis
without historical consciousness
without profundity of psychological type
something that would make my everyday life
insipid like a novel
stillborn like a motion picture
negative like a humorous anecdote
indifferent like a Renaissance painting
harmful like a political action and generally
servile and subjugated to the world's natural order
and the — commonly so-called — philanthropic sentiments.

A legislature
totally useless to the Authorities
would be a true deliverance.

The Antiphonist says:

THE HOLY INQUISITION

Mind you what pain subtracts from you
it adds it to you O Man
Soul sustained
who keeps boasting

Struggle as much as you wish
Perfection has no heels

And we need to go ahead
to fill all the Voids
if not then let's destroy ourselves drawing strength from the past.
There will come a time when we will sing upright
and brave to beauty.
Sooner or later
the birds will tame us

Let's go children . . .

True bravery
must be baptized in the sea
and bring back something of the sea breeze
to the eighth floors of the apartment houses,
must leave the battlefields
and grow in love and in the books
and emerge with another more beautiful name
and wait there
to be attacked and blasphemed
and bound with its hands behind and tried.

Each era with its Holy Inquisition.

The "void" exists
as long as you do not fall into it.

And Maria Nephele responds:

ST. FRANCIS OF ASSISI

What a pity that the Linguaphone of pleasure
has not yet been discovered!
Now that "nature" diminishes and the wind is rare
and men rot in woods entirely imaginary
it would be the loftiest wisdom if Saints reconciled
with their bodies
and heard again the angel's voice falling
like a fine spring rain
in the hour when knowledge of every kind is blazing . . .

Don't say: A justice will be found for us, too.
Don't expect anything from politics and science
The brand-new world is also the most ancient
turned inside out.

Don't labor in vain.

With my beauty I
will abolish the notion of the book;

I'll invent the new flowers
and pluck them from my bowels
and crown the public rose
king in the delta of my thighs.

From it will blow the wind
of true innocence
which few men will survive
yet all the birds
will be pecking the nipples of my breasts.

Each era with the St. Francis of its Assisi.

Try
to guide Technical perfection
to its natural state.

THE POET'S SONG

The first time on an island's soil
on November second at daybreak

I came out to see the world and regretted it
the "tight spot" as they say — I felt it instantly.

Nine months before my first day
I labored for my father's seed

and five hundred three in a row
afterward — against falsehood and poverty.

Difficult, difficult is the passage on earth
and it doesn't even come to anything.

I hid so much within myself
even I myself didn't know it.

Until one day driven by chance
I fell in love without any resistance

Yet even in the least thing I attempted
my dear fellows I always made a mess

first because I pursued the Unattainable
second because I was the kind that has no Double.

Whereupon cursing my luck
I came back to myself.

Maria Nephele says:

GOOD MORNING, GRIEF

Hello grief
Good morning grief
insect that lurks in me
and all night long lies in wait till I open my eye . . .

At first I've forgotten you;
I gaze at the lines of the ceiling —
suddenly you set foot and enter
consciousness.

You come to embitter the morning coffee,
to subtract something from the tiniest joy
of my hand at the window latch,
you bring disorder to the bath water,
provoke the first unpleasant telephone call
you're a monster
a microscopic Minotaur that seeks food
and is sustained with the slightest thing . . .

You eat eat Minotaur;
this is flesh not air
the way you're going nothing will remain.
Hello grief
Good morning grief
you've settled permanently within us
you're worse than viruses and bacilli,
philosophers examine you under the spectroscope
you've been the cause of a superb literature
we read it and "discover ourselves"
we suck our black candy

Ah let us be lost
wastrels of a fifth- or sixth-story happiness.

When misfortune is profitable
consider her a whore.

And the Antiphonist responds:

MORNING GYMNASTICS

An open window. Flower beds all around.
Straighten the body. Stretch out the hands.
One two three: my holy life
I reduce psychological strife.
Repeat. One two: I perceive my face
I appropriate my opposite.
Contraction one! Neither don'ts — nor nots.
Extend and bend the arms
in all directions;
up-side-forward-down:
give the dog the cat's due
                    give the cat the dog's.
Extend the head backward: ooonnneee
I accept no rule nnnooonnneee.
A deep breath: maiden O dainty maiden.
First principle: down with dexterity.

A leap forward four quick beats:
substitute the daily crimes.
One-two-three-four and repeat:
bravery is counterfeit.
Keep in tempo! Insist on Breton!
Attention hey! Study Fourier!

Turn the head to the left:
all is shit.
Turn the head to the right:
all is shit.
Position one! Conclusion none.
Fall out! Dismiss!
The girls kiss.

Take a leap
faster than decay.

Maria Nephele says:

THE POETS

What shall I do with you O my dear Poets
who for years feign the invincible souls

And for years wait for what I didn't wait for
standing in line like unclaimed articles . . .

What if they call you — none of you replies
outside is havoc, the world burns to the skies

Nothing, you demand — I wish I knew with what mind —
your rights over the void!

In times of wealth's adoration, O what indolence,
you exhale the vanity of ownership

Wrapped in Palm leaves you keep on carrying
the ill-fated and black-robed earthly Sphere

And you become in the stench of the hydrosulfate of mankind
the voluntary experimental animals of the Divine.

Man is attracted to God
as the shark to blood.

And the Antiphonist responds:

WHAT CONVINCES

Please notice my lips: the world depends on them.
On the correlations they dare and the unacceptable
similes, just as when on an evening that smells beautiful
we throw the Moon's woodcutter to the ground,
he bribes us with a bit of jasmine and we consent . . .

What convinces I maintain is like a chemical substance that alters.
Let a girl's cheek be beautiful,
all of us with eaten-away faces will return sometime from the Lands
of Truth.

Children I don't know how to explain this
but we need to be replaced by the old Bandits.
That we may direct our hand and it will go
there where a woman like an Apple Tree awaits half in the clouds
totally ignoring the distance that separates us.

And something else: when it starts raining
let us undress and shine like clover . . .

A mistaken sea cannot exist.

Maria Nephele says:

THE TWENTY-FOUR-HOUR LIFE

I was old at about eighteen
You'd say within twenty-four hours:
at eight o'clock I went to school studied played
by ten past ten I was perfected in foreign countries
(riding English and such)
then the first marriage, the trip,
by afternoon I was already bored;

from five to six a few mischiefs
at seven I remarried
at five past seven I was unfaithful
at eight I was already tired
cards receptions et cetera . . .

After dinner I looked into the mirror
in the other house, the big one
of my third, rich husband;
I saw light flowing and within it dolphins,
it seemed to me an echo of the other world
the poet's voice
Finland

Groenland

Erosland

I felt there was no longer time.
At midnight just as the hour calls for it
I committed the necessary murder.
Now I'm left with the cigarettes and the fire
of the night beside the dead.

When life fights,
the dead in Hades imitate the Medes.

And the Antiphonist responds:

THE LIFELONG MOMENT

Seize the lightning on your road,
O man; give it continuity; you can!
From the smell of grass from the heat of the sun
over the quicklime from the endless kiss
you should extract a century;

with a dome for beauty

and the echoing that
the angels bring to you in the basket,
the dew from your toils all fruit round
and red;

your anguish

full of keys that strike metallic in the wind,
or upright pipes that you blow like a harmonium
and you see all your trees gathering,
laurels and poplars the small and great
Marias whom no one touched but you;

all a single moment all your lone
lightning forever.
The sand with which you played as with your life the Luck
and the wreaths that time the powerless
enemy exchanged with your forever unknown maiden
if you have succeeded
once and for all to gaze straight into the light
it is the single moment
powerful over the abyss
the waterdrop itself

is Virtue

as the birds of Skiron and the sails of Argestes.

Years of light in the heavens
years of Virtue in quicklime.

Maria Nephele says:

SPEECH ON JUSTICE

Slowly very slowly in quicklime is Holy Tuesday consumed.
No wrinkle. Not even a tear.
Only the sun's wheel is heard like the "*Salva nos*"
   from the Monasteries
devouring decay
the hour when the women bring up from the well
that sound of the void
that we hear a little before disaster strikes us.

A hollowness like the palm's where our righteousness fits.

I loosened my hair before a wall
and at my side I lament a shadow of my shadow.

I sing and chant Man's Unwritten Words
I heaven's runaway who saw and saw.

I regret that my turn of speech is not the one
that befits our days
                                        Ladies and Gentlemen.
Nothing befits our days
and in addition I happen to be sad
just as when
                        you feel deeply tangible in your body
something for which you had till then only bad thoughts.
Let's stop joking then:
you'd kill a snake even if it wasn't wrong.

Such is our Justice!

Even the very very edge has its middle.

And the Antiphonist responds:

STUDY OF A NUDE

If you are of the Atreides go
elsewhere to shout aloud. Such fire doesn't kindle the sun
here where conscience rose and took on a maiden's real body
with flashes from the boundless valley —

Look: how memory ties the hair
back and lets the eyelids fall forward
trembling from so much truth;
how
the skin is taut at the shoulders and the loins;
something dazling where no one can ever
be brave or strong.
Just to exist.

Like blood. Like grapes. Man's long road
from the dark to the ever-shining,
touching finger after finger until the whole gulf
is explored and the enigma
the beautiful thighs keep tight is revealed;

the ineffable seashore from the lofty armpit to the soles of the feet.

Because it cannot be. The sailing all
around a body smooth young naked
ends there where another begins again. Like an undiscovered
rose of a maiden that is continually reborn
to erase the murder and appease the cries
of the victims; from the beginning of History to this day
a body smooth young naked: justice.

The Magellan of a rose
has yet to be born.

Maria Nephele says:

ELECTRA BAR

Two or three stairsteps under the surface
of the earth — and suddenly all the problems solved!
You hold the small world in a big crystal glass;
through the tiny ice cubes you see your fingernails colorful
faces that smile vaguely;
you see your Luck (but she has always turned her back)
a Megaera who wronged you and whom you never avenged . . .

Ah how clever of Erika
the flying hostess of Olympic Airways,
she passes high over the capital cities;
I must pass beneath them
beneath the sea monsters — beneath the fat well-fed bodies
if I'll ever be worthy (but again it is doubtful)
of that vein in which Agamemnon's blood still flows
with no more help from an unknown brother —

Give me another gin fizz.

How lovely it is when the mind blurs — then the Heroes kill
in make-believe just as in the movies
you delight in blood; the hour when real blood
gushes forth on the stairsteps
you touch it with the finger and the curse awakens in you
the Queen with the cobwebs,
her eyes unbeatable and full of darkness;
shorn and ugly, I graze the swine
for centuries now, outside the walls
I wait for the message — the first rooster in Hades
something like the saxophone with a celestial clarity
little girls running riding on rubber dragons.

The Earth just now is revealed in its true size.
Zeus thunders

And the Antiphonist responds:

PARTHENOGENESIS

Flax plants
flax plants and maples
mushrooms and strawflowers
innocent little girls of the rain where have you conceived me?
There? In the third height? From the pollen of invisible gardens?
I am, then. I confirm this. I.
Yes for there I was born for there I was announced by the light
that gave you this power of lightning.

Why had I not died long ago when I could have
seen like fish leaping from the sea
the one that was indeed the
real earth.
This I want to see and dwell in it
the sea-purple and marvelous in beauty the golden
the white the one whiter than chalk or snow . . .

Raise me amid the revolving
small wheels of the ethers and leave me
in the inundations of citrus fruits lest from one
to the other body my weight be changed
into a dazzling radiance around innocent beings
that I alone yearned for and no one else.

Flax plants
flax plants and maples
bluets and periwinkles
spearmint and wild daisies
innocent little girls of the rain reserve a place for me
on the right side of spring from this time on there
in the third height; in midair
I go — and with their puffed cheeks
the boys your husbands blow — I keep on
with the mountain ridges carved on my chest

Maria Nephele says:

darkness
Zeus thunders
this is neither defeat nor victory.
Let us the entombed dare something else.

Whoever can electrify solitude
still has humanity within himself.

And the Antiphonist responds:

the sunspot in my hair
the dragnet of the sea in my one hand . . .

Alpha: ageless time
Beta: bright-lightning Zeus
Gamma: landless me.

If something grows impatient in the wild mint
it is the hound of your sanctity.

Maria Nephele says:

DJENDA

90% of whatever
misfortune contains us.
The present is nonexistent and half
of my hair is already elsewhere
it waves in other epochs.

Half-houses in midair
ruins of old cities I've never known
pieces of Sardis and Persepolis
Corinth Alexandria;
the ancient temples with the stone floors and the heavy
sandals of the priests
the incense offerings
under the bare breasts and the noise of brass links
the hour of dancing, tatters,
motley patches, my soul,
just like the wide skirts I've been wearing lately
montgolfier of regrets
and the casual phrases in the street:
"What do you bring?" "Gold." "Cheer."

I "bring" nothing
nor do they "bring" to me
I teach with my body the bone of the sea
the blue coral with the transparencies
I walk sundered in the window and endlessly draw
sky under my feet; I cast down the bucket
to bring up jasmine and aster;
according to the time I'm called Tryphera or Anemone
sometimes even Djenda
how beautiful
I understand nothing.

Djenda nonexistent word
self-same brand of electric bulbs

And the Antiphonist responds:

ICH SEHE DICH

Patches of oceans *Ich sehe dich*
Maria *in tausend Bildern*
of light and iodine and LAIT INNOXA
and sideways your hands over the cord.
You are the new Lachesis. You telephone
to end my service on earth. Don't worry
I'm already dying from celestial starvation.

Mythical fish I see passing
over my head the air burns
SWISSAIR BEA TWA
Ah my Nereids I'll never be worthy
of seeing my name printed
DIE WELT TIMES FIGARO
but behind death with a mane
KODAK PHILIPS OLIVETTI
shining the stallion awaits me
to cross over the barrier to cross over the barrier
of the sound of obscurity I
JAGUAR CHEVROLET PEUGEOT
the glass will stop on your lips and
JOHNNIE WALKER CINZANO PERRIER
earthly vainglory will be superfluous for you
only poetry only poetry
SAAB MERCEDES FERRARI
shredding the façades of old houses
NESCAFÉ LINGUAPHONE
like covers of periodicals where all
PARKER WATERMAN BIC
the beautiful maidens of a single day have appeared once
rosecolored like the girl
of ELIZABETH ARDEN and NINA RICCI.

Maria puma of the public streets
in the diaphanous nylon or dralon

Maria Nephele says:

half-Sanskrit half-Celtic
Djenda the trembling
image of mine magnified in the hands of the peoples
Djenda cultural revolution
Djenda I six thousand years ago
with my side on the mountains of Crete
pointing
to the huge inequality
that will spread to divide the world

Djenda, I who took time not to wrong
Djenda.

A *naked body is the only extension of the intelligible line*
that unites us with the mysterious.

And the Antiphonist responds:

half the ashes that burn
PHILIP MORRIS   KENT   CRAVEN A
and half the nerve-racking exhaust
MOBILOIL   SHELL   BP
in our soul's boundless Arizona
steppe of the most terrible winter
you'll raise a stentorian cry
the cry of the wounded animal

O Maria Nephele the beautiful
O Maria Nephele the heraldic.

Somewhere between Tuesday and Wednesday
your real day must have been misplaced.

Maria Nephele says:

STALIN

Flickering I'll transcribe my orbit
over the cathedrals and the castles
of old crowned kings like that radiance
once over Bethlehem.

Yes my pale face
my long hair the magi know them.
For them they talk — for this heaven-sent maiden
who in peace consented to say: beware
t h e m a n y c o u n t e r f e i t t h e O n e.

If I am she it doesn't matter;
a voice must be automatic and repetitive
like a gun with a range that covers centuries;
and I derive from the Mongols
I arrive like the Trans-Siberian
with my own small light and a laurel branch in my hand.

I say it then although it's not worth a dime
since it was suggested to me by the rhyme.

Before the One has time to make me alter,
before he imposes a "brand-new order"
I repeat and say good-bye to you — I go to a prison cell:
a moon belongs to America as well
but a soul that is not sold — to Matala or Katmandu.

Each era with its Stalin, too.

When you hear "order"
human flesh smells.

And the Antiphonist responds:

THE HUNGARIAN UPRISING

You heard the maiden's words:
the One counterfeits the many.

In keeping with the times he puts on the chiton
of the General and is proclaimed "by roaring" in the Agora
the Supreme
Archon who wears the splendid purple robe
with scepter and crown by the grace of God
who blesses with tiara and miter — who in the name
of the Party and the People advances with gun barrels and tanks

(and you my swallow — go tweet-tweet if you dare!)

until the Body of the Army and the Body of Man
become as the theory has wished it — One.
Above all, expediency
arrives also from on high like an angel of Rublev
it is a monster;
what the true light is no one knows.

Maria Nephele, beware — turn the machine gun this way
and all of you armed
dwarves of fairy-tale witches and wild beasts
women men with hoes pick-axes
stones from the pavement gas pumps carriages
at him!
(O Maiden You told me so)

Each era with its Hungarian Uprising.

If you are destined to die, die but take care
to become the first rooster in Hades.

THE ETERNAL WAGER

1

That one day you shall bite into the new lemon
and release
huge quantities of sun from inside it.

2

That all the currents of the seas
suddenly illumined will reveal you
raising the storm to the moral level.

3

That even in your death you shall be again
like water in the sun
that turns cold by instinct.

4

That you shall be catechized by the birds
and a foliage of words will clothe you
in Greek so you shall seem invincible.

5

That a waterdrop will culminate
imperceptibly on your eyelashes
beyond pain and after many tears.

6

That all the world's heartlessness will turn to stone
so you can sit regally
with an obedient bird in your palm.

7

That alone at last you shall be united
slowly with the grandeur
of sunrise and of sunset.

NOTES

NOTES

page

vii *"In it a girl":* From "Odysseus Elytis on His Poetry," an interview with Ivar Ivask, *Books Abroad,* vol. 49, Autumn 1975, p. 638.

vii *"I met this young woman":* Ibid., p. 640.

viii *"I try to understand":* Ibid.

x *"It is a Paradise":* Odysseus Elytis, *Anoihta Hartia* (Athens: Asterias, 1974), p. 34.

xi *"the tendency toward":* Ibid., p. 32.

xiii *"the common trait":* Ibid., p. 18.

xiii *"I personally believe":* Ibid., p. 17.

xiii *"the lack of fantasy":* Ibid.

xiii *"a source of innocence":* From "Odysseus Elytis on His Poetry," *Books Abroad,* p. 643. The reader should also consult two other books of Elytis available in English translation, *The Sovereign Sun: Selected Poems by Odysseus Elytis,* translated by Kimon Friar (Philadelphia: Temple University Press, 1974), and the *Axion Esti,* translated by Edmund Keeley and George Savidis (Pittsburgh: University of Pittsburgh Press, 1974).

xiv *"That's why I write":* Elytis, *Anoihta Hartia,* p. 43.

xv *"Divine, toil, feel":* From "The Concert of the Hyacinth," in *Orientations* (Athens: Ikaros, 1939).

1 *M.N.:* Maria Nephele.

1 A.: Antiphonist. A person who sings a hymn, verse, or prayer in alternate parts, responding to another voice.

1 *"like the Bishops":* Bishops of the Eastern Orthodox Church are buried seated upright, rather than in a horizontal position.

2 ΑΡΙΜΝΑ ΕΦΗ ΕΛ: An anagram for Maria Nephele and an allusion to the anagram for the name Marina, as it appears in the *Axion Esti.* Marina is a permanent persona in Elytis's mythical world.

6 *Baobab . . . Uncarabo:* names of trees in imitation of Latin words, whose derivations and sounds suggest roughness, ferocity, and cannibalism.

7 *boustrophedon:* A method of writing used by the ancient Greeks, with lines inscribed alternately from right to left and from left to right, like the course of oxen ploughing in successive rows.

7 *Light-Tree:* A frequent image in Elytis's poetry and the title of a major volume of his work published in 1971.

9 *spreading the fingers:* A palm stretched forward with spread fingers is an insult or curse for modern Greeks. A palm turned inward with spread fingers suggests the shape of a star. The poet was inspired by a production in Paris of Paul Claudel's *Le Partage du Midi,* in which Jean-Louis Barrault ended the performance by raising his right hand ceremoniously, forming a star.

10 *Nephelegeretes:* A Homeric epithet for Zeus, meaning "the cloud-gatherer." It appears frequently in both the *Iliad* and the *Odyssey.*

page

12 *"Come!"*: From Revelation 6:1 ff.

13 *destined to suffer:* Ibid., 2:10 ff.

15 *the seven deep furrows:* A paraphrase taken from Revelation 1:16 ff.

15 *"the Destroyer"*: Refers to Abaddon, or Apollyon, in Revelation 9:11.

16 *Das Reine . . . Allerunnatürlichste:* "The pure can reveal itself only in the impure, and you try to express the noble without any ordinariness and thus it becomes the most unnatural of all things." A quotation from Friedrich Hölderlin (1770–1843), in his letter (number 167) to Christian Ludwig Neuffer, November 12, 1798. Friedrich Hölderlin, *Sämtliche Werke und Briefe,* vol. 4 (Berlin: Aufbau-Verlag, 1970), p. 323.

17 *The Waterdrop:* A recurrent motif in Elytis's poetry and especially prominent in his collection *Exi Kai Mia Typseis Yia Ton Ouranon,* published in 1960.

17 *Athos:* Mt. Athos, the Holy Mountain in northern Greece that is home to twenty independent monasteries of the Eastern Orthodox Church.

18 *cloudy Sunday:* Refers to a popular Greek song written by Vasilis Tsitsanis in 1944, during the German occupation.

18 *Theotokopoulos:* Dominikos Theotokopoulos, or El Greco (1541–1614), the Spanish painter born in Crete.

18 *"Asterobadon" "Idiolathes" "Mikyon"*: Names imitating those of angels of the Old Testament or the Apocrypha.

19 *Aegeïs:* A legendary island in the Aegean Sea identified with lost Atlantis.

19 *King Evenor:* The King of Atlantis. Plato, *Critias,* 111c.

20 *The martyrdom of St. Maurice:* Refers to a painting by El Greco at the monastery of Escorial near Madrid.

22 *Thunderbolt Steers:* Refers to an apothegm of the sixth-century-B.C. Ionian philosopher Heraclitus. Fragment 64, in H. Diehls, *Die Fragmente der Vorsokratiker,* sixth edition (Berlin, 1934).

23 *Léonor Fini:* Italian artist (1908–   ) of the Paris school whose work is characterized by an intense dreamlike quality.

23 *Tra un fiore:* "Between one flower plucked and another inexpressible nothing." From the poem "Eterno," by Giuseppe Ungaretti (1888–1970), in his collection *L'Allegria* (Milan: Preda, 1934).

25 *Lambda:* The eleventh book of the *Iliad,* pivotal to the development of the poem's plot. It contains the wounding of the Greek heroes Agamemnon, Diomedes, and Odysseus, and begins the sequence of events leading to Patroklos's death and Achilles' return to the battlefield.

28 *"it's meaningless"*: A line from Elytis's poem "The Clepsydrae of the Unknown," in *Prosanatolismoi* (Athens: Ikaros, 1939).

30 *Tahiti:* A restaurant in Saint-Tropez.

33 *You're the man:* An allusion to the myth of Agamemnon's slaying.

34 *Lasithi:* A plateau in central Crete covered with small windmills.

34 *Sathes and Merione:* The male and female genital organs mentioned

page

by sixth-century-B.C. poet Archilochus, Fragment 68; and by eleventh-century poet Rufinus, Fragment 36, in *The Greek Anthology*, Vol. 1, Book V. Edited by E. H. Warmington. Loeb Classical Library (Cambridge: Harvard University Press).

38 *"Without sighs or fear"*: A line from *Philokalia, a* codex of mystical prayers of the Church Fathers, compiled by Nikodemus of Mt. Athos in the eighteenth century.

39 *"Without limits without terms"*: A line from "The Arrows," a poem by Andreas Empeirikos (1901–1975) in *Endohora* (Athens: Ikaros, 1945).

40 *The Upper Tarquinia:* Ancient city of the Etruscans, northwest of Rome. Elytis contrasts the Etruscan visual sensibility as shown in their third-century-B.C. grave frescoes to that of Renaissance art, represented by paintings in the Pitti Palace in Florence.

41 *The Eye of the Locust:* The locust's eye breaks the field of vision into many separate planes. To emphasize the feeling of a fragmented perception, Elytis has divided the poem into seven seemingly unrelated parts; yet the first lines of each part form a uniform, meaningful phrase that enhances the whole poem.

41 *Sophie von Kühn:* Fiancée of the German poet Novalis (1771–1801). She died at age fourteen, plunging the poet into grief.

44 *Pandrosou Street:* A narrow street in Plaka, the old section of Athens at the foot of the Acropolis.

44 *Voie lactée ô soeur lumineuse:* "O milky way, luminous sister." A line from "La Chanson du Mal Aimé," a poem from *Alcools* (Paris: Mercure de France, 1913) by Guillaume Apollinaire (1880–1918).

45 *en las purpureas horas:* "in the purple hours." A line from "Fábula de Polifemo y Galatea," by Luis Góngora y Argote (1561–1627).

46 *Let's go children:* From Aeschylus, *Persians,* 1.402.

51 *Fourier:* French Utopian philosopher (1772–1837).

54 *Finland:* From "About This," a poem by Vladimir Mayakovsky (1893–1930), in *Mayakovsky,* edited by Herbert Marshall (New York: Hill & Wang, 1965).

55 *Skiron:* Northwest wind.

55 *Argestes:* South wind.

58 *Electra Bar:* Name of a night club, alluding to the myth of Electra and the mechanism of revenge.

59 *the sea-purple:* From Plato, *Phaedo,* 110C.

62 *"What do you bring?"*: From an anonymous poem in *The Greek Anthology*, Vol. 1, Book V, Fragment 101.

62 *Tryphera or Anemone:* Names of courtesans who appear in love poems in *The Greek Anthology*.

63 *Ich sehe dich . . . :* "I see you in thousands of images." From Novalis's "Geistliche Lieder," No. XV., a poem he addresses to the Holy Virgin, in *Schriften,* edited by Paul Kluckhohn and Richard Samuel. 4 vols. (Leipzig, 1929).

63 LAIT INNOXA: The trademarks of multinational companies form

page

a modern heraldry comparable to the blazons of Renaissance nobility.

66 *Matala:* A village on the southern coast of Crete, near Phaestos and Agia Triada.

67 *an angel of Rublev:* An icon by the Russian painter Andrew Rublev (1370–1425) in the State Tretyakov Gallery in Moscow.

67 O *maiden:* A paraphrased line from "The Poisoned Maiden," by Dionysios Solomos (1798–1857), the national poet of Greece, in his collection *Poiemata* (Athens: Ikaros, 1961).